THIS

Thanks giving

Planner Belongs To:

_____

Dedication

This Thanksgiving Planner book is dedicated to all the energetic and hard working people out there who love to plan a memorable Thanksgiving and want to document the process.

You are my inspiration for producing books and I'm honored to be a part of keeping all of your Thanksgiving notes and records organized.

This journal notebook will help you record your details about your Thanksgiving plan.

Thoughtfully put together with these sections to record: Contact Page, 3 Weeks Before Checklist, Thanksgiving Week Checklist, Kitchen Checklist, Photos, Cleaning Checklist, Menu Planner, Cooking Schedule, Table & Decor Seating, Guest List & much, much more.

How to Use this Book

The purpose of this book is to keep all of your Thanksgiving notes all in one place. It will help keep you organized.

This Thanksgiving Journal will allow you to accurately document every detail about your Thanksgiving plan. It's a great way to chart your course through a memorable Thanskgiving.

Here are examples of the prompts for you to fill in and write about your experience in this book:

1. Contact Page
2. 3 Weeks Before Checklist - Detailed checklist of what you need to do 3 weeks in advance, from creating a guest list, gathering Thanksgiving recipe/ recipes, to declutter countertops, and much, much more.
3. Thanksgiving Week Checklist - Detailed checklist of things you need to do the week of Thanksgiving, from move the turkey from the freezer to the fridge, confirm guest list, set the table, shop perishables and much, much more.
4. Kitchen Checklist - Detailed checklist of essentials, kitchen tools & bakeware.
5. October & November Monthly Calendar Overview - Undated October & November calendars to fill in schedules, appointments, errands, etc.
6. Photos - Plenty of pages to glue, tape or paste your photographs.
7. Thanksgiving Week Planner - Space for you to write you agenda that is specific to your situation.
8. Cleaning Checklist - Detailed checklist to clean Kitchen, Dining Room, Living/ Family Room, Guest Room, Entry/ Front Porch, & Bathrooms.
9. Shopping List & Grocery List - Detailed shopping list for you to fill in on shopping for Decorations, Table Linens & Accessories, Kitchen Items, Table & Bar Items, Non-Perishables, Household & Paper Goods. Also a blank Grocery List for you to fill in.
10. Budget Tracker - Record the Item, Budgeted, Actual & Difference.
11. Menu Planner - Space to write out your menu including Appetizers, Main Course, Side Dishes, Casseroles, Drinks, Desserts and Shopping List.
12. Thanksgiving Day Cooking Schedule - Hour by hour schedule for you to fill in with your tasks and agenda.
13. Cooking Time Table - Detailed list for you to record for each menu item: Menu Item, Cook Method, Ready Time, Cook Time, Begin Cook, Prep Time, Begin Prep.
14. Table Decor & Seating - Detailed checklist for your table: # of Tables, # of Chairs, Formal/ Informal, Table Cloth, Table Runner, Napkins, Napkin Rings, Vases, Place Cards, Candlesticks, Candles, Diagram of Informal Setting, Diagram of Formal Setting, and Space to sketch Seating Arrangement.
15. Guest List - Record Guest Name, Bringing, Requests, Adults, Children & RSVP checkbox.
16. Memories Pages - Space to write your memories that you will cherish and love to look back & reflect on from year to year.
17. Notes - Blank lined notes for writing any additional information you like, such as everyone's gratitude for each day, what worked, what didn't work, etc.

Enjoy!

Thanksgiving *checklist*

Getting Organized

- ○ Put all activities and appointments on the calendar.
- ○ Set a budget for hosting Thanksgiving dinner.
- ○ Create your guest list and invite your guests.
- ○ Set RSVP date at least 10 days before Thanksgiving.

Plan The Menu

- ○ Gather favorite Thanksgiving recipes and new recipes to try.
- ○ Decide if you will make the entire meal yourself or ask guests to bring a dish.
- ○ Plan your menu and create a comprehensive list of ingredients you'll need.

Preparing Your Kitchen

- ○ Start a shopping list for all the food and supplies you'll need.
- ○ Declutter countertops to make room for food preparations.
- ○ Organize and inventory your pantry and freezer.
- ○ Stock up on seasonal baking and cooking ingredients.

Preparing Your Home

- ○ Plan your table décor and centerpiece. Take inventory of linens and accessories.
- ○ Declutter and deep clean your dining room.
- ○ Take stock of table and bar items using the checklist.
- ○ Plan your Thanksgiving decor. Inspect candles and other decorations.
- ○ Make a list of worn-out decorations or new décor to purchase.
- ○ Take care of any home maintenance issues or "spruce up" areas in need.

Notes

Notes

Thanksgiving *checklist*

Sunday/Monday

- ○ Confirm guest attendance and food contributions.
- ○ Wash all cookware and serving pieces that you haven't used recently.
- ○ Label serving dishes with intended menu item.
- ○ Tidy up living and dining rooms. Finish decorating.
- ○ Thoroughly clean the bathroom guests will be using.
- ○ Iron table linens and polish silver.
- ○

Tuesday

- ○ Move the turkey to the refrigerator to defrost.
- ○ Place the turkey in the coldest area with a pan underneath to catch drips.
- ○ Move frozen dishes to the refrigerator.
- ○ Make cranberry sauce, breads, rolls, and pie crusts.
- ○ Clean vegetables and refrigerate. Store in sealed plastic bag.
- ○ Finalize your cooking schedule for Thursday.
- ○ Shop for perishable groceries, fresh flowers, and remaining items.
- ○ Do a spot cleaning of entertaining rooms.
- ○ Make space for guest's coats and shoes.
- ○

Wednesday

- ○ Make your pies and other desserts.
- ○ Make side dishes that will reheat well.
- ○ Prep any vegetables, toppings, garnishes and stuffing ingredients.
- ○ Set up the bar and chill the wine.
- ○ Set the dining table. Arrange the chairs.
- ○ Set out flowers, candles and other decorations.
- ○

Notes

Kitchen *checklist*

Turkey Essentials

○	Roasting Pan	○	Oven Thermometer
○	Roasting Rack	○	Meat Thermometer
○	Carving Set	○	Bulb Baster
○	Carving Board	○	Flavor Injector
○	Cheesecloth	○	Turkey Lifters
○	Brining Bags	○	Fine Mesh Strainer
○	Butcher's Twine	○	Gravy Separator
○		○	

Kitchen Tools

○	Saucepans	○	Dry Measuring cups
○	Wooden spoon	○	Liquid Measuring cups
○	Slotted spoon	○	Grater
○	Flat Whisk	○	Colander
○	Paring knife	○	Potato masher
○	Vegetable Peeler	○	Food Processor
○	Tongs	○	Blender
○	Mandoline Slicer	○	Stand Mixer
○		○	Hand Mixer
○		○	

Bakeware

○	Pie Dishes	○	Hand sifter
○	Casserole Dishes	○	Rolling pin
○	Baking Sheets	○	Oven Mitts
○	Wire Cooling Racks	○	Apron
○	Mixing Bowls	○	Pie Server
○	Spatulas	○	
○		○	

Shopping List

○	
○	
○	
○	
○	
○	
○	
○	
○	
○	
○	
○	
○	
○	
○	
○	
○	
○	
○	
○	
○	
○	
○	
○	
○	

Notes

Table & Bar checklist

Dinnerware

○	Dinner Plates	○	Bowls
○	Bread Plates	○	Cups and Saucers
○	Salad/Dessert Plates	○	Chargers
○		○	

Drinkware

○	Red Wine Glasses	○	Water Glasses
○	White Wine Glasses	○	Highball Glasses
○	Wine Carafe	○	Water Pitcher
○	Cork Screw	○	Bar Tool Set
○	Wine Stoppers	○	Coasters
○	Ice Bucket	○	

Flatware

○	5 piece Settings	○	Steak Knives
○	Serving Spoons	○	Chef's Knife
○	Serving Forks	○	Bread Knife
○	Ladle	○	Cheese Knife
○	Dessert Server	○	

Serving

○	Turkey Platter	○	Trivets
○	Serving Bowls	○	Butter Dish
○	Serving Platters	○	Gravy Boat
○	Salad Bowl	○	Bread Basket
○	Soup Tureen	○	Sugar & Creamer Set
○	Serving Trays	○	Salt & Pepper Shakers
○	Condiment Dishes	○	Cheese Board
○		○	
○		○	

Shopping List

○	
○	
○	
○	
○	
○	
○	
○	
○	
○	
○	
○	
○	
○	
○	
○	
○	
○	
○	
○	
○	
○	
○	
○	
○	

Notes

October

Sunday	Monday	Tuesday	Wednesday	Thursday	Friday	Saturday

Notes

October

Sunday	Monday	Tuesday	Wednesday	Thursday	Friday	Saturday

Notes

October

Sunday	Monday	Tuesday	Wednesday	Thursday	Friday	Saturday

Notes

Thanks giving

Notes

November

Sunday	Monday	Tuesday	Wednesday	Thursday	Friday	Saturday

Notes

_____

_____

_____

_____

_____

November

Sunday	Monday	Tuesday	Wednesday	Thursday	Friday	Saturday

Notes

_____

_____

_____

_____

_____

_____

November

Sunday	Monday	Tuesday	Wednesday	Thursday	Friday	Saturday

Notes

thanks.
giving

Notes

Thanksgiving Week *planner*

Friday	Saturday	Sunday

Monday	Tuesday	Wednesday

Thursday	Notes	Give Thanks

Notes

Thanksgiving Week *planner*

Friday	Saturday	Sunday

Monday	Tuesday	Wednesday

Thursday	Notes	Give Thanks

Notes

Thanksgiving Week *planner*

Friday	Saturday	Sunday

Monday	Tuesday	Wednesday

Thursday	Notes	Give Thanks

Notes

Thanksgiving Week *planner*

Friday	Saturday	Sunday

Monday	Tuesday	Wednesday

Thursday	Notes	Give Thanks

Notes

Thanksgiving Week *planner*

Friday	Saturday	Sunday

Monday	Tuesday	Wednesday

Thursday	Notes	Give Thanks

Notes

Thanks giving

Weekly agenda

Schedule

Monday

Tuesday

Wednesday

Thursday

Friday

Saturday

Sunday

To-Do

Notes

Notes

Weekly agenda

Schedule

☐ Monday

☐ Tuesday

☐ Wednesday

☐ Thursday

☐ Friday

☐ Saturday

☐ Sunday

To-Do

Notes

Notes

Weekly agenda

Schedule

☐ Monday

☐ Tuesday

☐ Wednesday

☐ Thursday

☐ Friday

☐ Saturday

☐ Sunday

To-Do

Notes

Notes

Weekly agenda

Schedule

☐ Monday

☐ Tuesday

☐ Wednesday

☐ Thursday

☐ Friday

☐ Saturday

☐ Sunday

To-Do

Notes

Notes

Weekly agenda

Schedule

☐ Monday

☐ Tuesday

☐ Wednesday

☐ Thursday

☐ Friday

☐ Saturday

☐ Sunday

To-Do

Notes

Notes

Four Week checklist

Week 1	Week 2	Week 3

Week 4

Sunday	Monday	Tuesday	Wednesday

Thanksgiving Day

Morning	Midday	1 Hour Before Dinner

Notes

Four Week checklist

Week 1	Week 2	Week 3

Week 4			
Sunday	Monday	Tuesday	Wednesday

Thanksgiving Day		
Morning	Midday	1 Hour Before Dinner

Notes

Four Week *checklist*

Week 1	Week 2	Week 3

Week 4			
Sunday	Monday	Tuesday	Wednesday

Thanksgiving Day		
Morning	Midday	1 Hour Before Dinner

Notes

Four Week *checklist*

Week 1	Week 2	Week 3

Week 4			
Sunday	Monday	Tuesday	Wednesday

Thanksgiving Day		
Morning	Midday	1 Hour Before Dinner

Notes

Four Week checklist

Week 1	Week 2	Week 3

Week 4

Sunday	Monday	Tuesday	Wednesday

Thanksgiving Day

Morning	Midday	1 Hour Before Dinner

Notes

Thanks giving

Cleaning *checklist*

Kitchen

- ◯ Wipe down lights fixtures and fans.
- ◯ Wipe down the cabinets.
- ◯ Clean out refrigerator and freezer.
- ◯ Clean microwave, stove, and oven.
- ◯ Clear and clean counters.
- ◯ Wipe down appliances.
- ◯ Clean and organize pantry.
- ◯ Sweep and mop the floor.
- ◯
- ◯
- ◯

Dining Room

- ◯ Wipe off marks on doors and walls.
- ◯ Clean light fixtures and fans.
- ◯ Wipe down mirrors and glass.
- ◯ Dust furniture and decor.
- ◯ Wipe down and polish table.
- ◯ Wipe down chairs.
- ◯ Wipe down baseboards.
- ◯ Vacuum and/or mop the floor.
- ◯
- ◯
- ◯

Living/Family Rooms

- ◯ Wipe off marks on doors and walls.
- ◯ Clean light fixtures and fans.
- ◯ Wipe down mirrors and glass.
- ◯ Dust furniture and decor.
- ◯ Wipe down electronics.
- ◯ Wipe down baseboards.
- ◯ Vacuum and/or mop the floor.
- ◯

Guest Room

- ◯ Change and wash linens.
- ◯ Dust furniture and decor.
- ◯ Wipe down mirrors and glass.
- ◯ Vacuum and mop the floor.
- ◯ Add a special touch to welcome guests.
- ◯

Bathrooms

- ◯ Wash shower curtains and rugs.
- ◯ Scrub shower, sink, and toilet
- ◯ Wipe down mirrors and glass.
- ◯ Wipe down counters.
- ◯ Put out fresh towels and candles.
- ◯ Stock with extra soap and toilet paper.
- ◯ Sweep and mop floor.
- ◯

Entry/Front Porch

- ◯ Clear any cobwebs and leaves.
- ◯ Wipe down the doorframe.
- ◯ Clean light fixtures and glass.
- ◯ Shake door mat.
- ◯ Hang a seasonal wreath on the front door.
- ◯

Shopping *list*

Decorations

Table Linens & Accessories

Kitchen Items

Table & Bar Items

Non-Perishables

Household & Paper Goods

Notes

Shopping list

Decorations

Table Linens & Accessories

Kitchen Items

Table & Bar Items

None-Perishables

Household & Paper Goods

Notes

Shopping list

Decorations

Table Linens & Accessories

Kitchen Items

Table & Bar Items

None-Perishables

Household & Paper Goods

Notes

Grocery list

Notes

Grocery list

Notes

Grocery *list*

Notes

Grocery list

Notes

Grocery list

Notes

Budget tracker

Item	Budgeted	Actual	Difference

Budget tracker

Item	Budgeted	Actual	Difference

Budget tracker

Item	Budgeted	Actual	Difference

Budget tracker

Item	Budgeted	Actual	Difference

Budget tracker

Item	Budgeted	Actual	Difference

Notes

Cooking plan

Main Course:

Ingredients List:

Appetizers & Sides

Desserts:

Drinks:

Cooking plan

Main Course:

_____
_____
_____
_____
_____

Appetizers & Sides

_____
_____
_____
_____
_____
_____
_____
_____
_____
_____
_____

Desserts:

_____
_____
_____
_____

Drinks:

_____
_____
_____
_____

Ingredients List:

_____
_____
_____
_____
_____
_____
_____
_____
_____
_____
_____
_____
_____
_____
_____
_____
_____
_____
_____
_____
_____
_____
_____
_____
_____
_____
_____
_____
_____
_____
_____
_____

Cooking *plan*

Main Course:

Appetizers & Sides

Desserts:

Drinks:

Ingredients List:

Cooking *plan*

Main Course:

Appetizers & Sides

Desserts:

Drinks:

Ingredients List:

Cooking plan

Main Course:

Appetizers & Sides

Desserts:

Drinks:

Ingredients List:

Notes

Menu planner

MENU

Appetizers

Main Course

Side Dishes

Casseroles

Drinks

Desserts

Shopping list

Notes

Menu planner

MENU	Shopping list

Appetizers

Main Course

Side Dishes

Casseroles

Drinks

Desserts

Notes

Menu planner

MENU

Appetizers

Main Course

Side Dishes

Casseroles

Drinks

Desserts

Shopping list

Notes

Menu planner

Appetizers

Main Course

Side Dishes

Casseroles

Drinks

Desserts

Notes

Menu planner

Appetizers

Main Course

Side Dishes

Casseroles

Drinks

Desserts

Notes

Master Ingredient list

☐	☐
☐	☐
☐	☐
☐	☐
☐	☐
☐	☐
☐	☐
☐	☐
☐	☐
☐	☐
☐	☐
☐	☐
☐	☐
☐	☐
☐	☐
☐	☐
☐	☐
☐	☐
☐	☐
☐	☐
☐	☐
☐	☐
☐	☐
☐	☐
☐	☐

Master Ingredient *list*

☐	☐
☐	☐
☐	☐
☐	☐
☐	☐
☐	☐
☐	☐
☐	☐
☐	☐
☐	☐
☐	☐
☐	☐
☐	☐
☐	☐
☐	☐
☐	☐
☐	☐
☐	☐
☐	☐
☐	☐
☐	☐
☐	☐
☐	☐
☐	☐
☐	☐

Master Ingredient list

Master Ingredient *list*

Master Ingredient *list*

Thanksgiving Day Cooking
schedule

Thanksgiving meal served at:

Time	What Needs To Be Done?
7:00 a.m.	
8:00 a.m.	
9:00 a.m.	
10:00 a.m.	
11:00 a.m.	
12:00 p.m.	
1:00 p.m.	
2:00 p.m.	
3:00 p.m.	
4:00 p.m.	
5:00 p.m.	
6:00 p.m.	
7:00 p.m.	
8:00 p.m.	
9:00 p.m.	

Thanksgiving Day Cooking
schedule

Thanksgiving meal served at:

Time	What Needs To Be Done?
7:00 a.m.	
8:00 a.m.	
9:00 a.m.	
10:00 a.m.	
11:00 a.m.	
12:00 p.m.	
1:00 p.m.	
2:00 p.m.	
3:00 p.m.	
4:00 p.m.	
5:00 p.m.	
6:00 p.m.	
7:00 p.m.	
8:00 p.m.	
9:00 p.m.	

Thanksgiving Day Cooking
schedule

Thanksgiving meal served at:

Time	What Needs To Be Done?
7:00 a.m.	
8:00 a.m.	
9:00 a.m.	
10:00 a.m.	
11:00 a.m.	
12:00 p.m.	
1:00 p.m.	
2:00 p.m.	
3:00 p.m.	
4:00 p.m.	
5:00 p.m.	
6:00 p.m.	
7:00 p.m.	
8:00 p.m.	
9:00 p.m.	

Notes

Thanks-
giving

Cooking Time *table*

Dinner Time:		Guests:		Turkey LBS:		Cook Time:

Menu Item	Cook Method	Ready Time	Cook Time	Begin Cook	Prep Time	Begin Prep

Cooking Time *table*

Dinner Time:		Guests:		Turkey LBS:		Cook Time:

Menu Item	Cook Method	Ready Time	Cook Time	Begin Cook	Prep Time	Begin Prep

Cooking Time *table*

Dinner Time:		Guests:		Turkey LBS:		Cook Time:

Menu Item	Cook Method	Ready Time	Cook Time	Begin Cook	Prep Time	Begin Prep

Notes

Table, Décor & seating

The Dining Table

Tables: #	Chairs: #	○ Formal ○ Informal

Linens & Accessories

		Centerpiece
○ Table cloth	○ Vases	
○ Table runner	○ Place Cards	
○ Napkins	○ Candlesticks	
○ Napkin Rings	○ Candles	

Other Table Décor

Informal

Water glass
Wineglass
Plate
Napkin
Salad fork
Dinner fork
Dinner knife
Teaspoon
Soup spoon

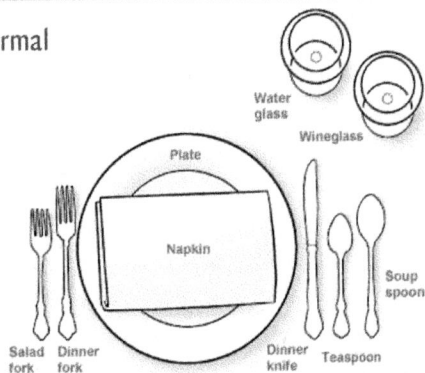

Utensils are placed one inch from the edge of the table

Formal

Place card
Water glass
Wineglass (red)
Wineglass (white)
Bread plate
Dessert spoon
Cake fork
Bread knife
Service plate
Salad plate
Napkin
Salad fork
Dinner fork
Dinner knife
Teaspoon
Soup spoon
Cup and saucer generally aren't placed on the table until the dessert course

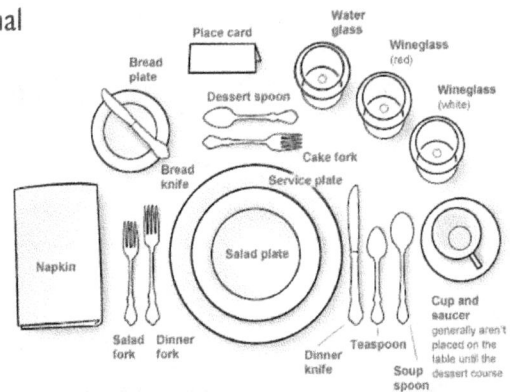

Seating Arrangement

Notes

Thanks giving

Guest list

RSVP	Guest	Bringing	Requests	Adults	Children
☐					
☐					
☐					
☐					
☐					
☐					
☐					
☐					
☐					
☐					
☐					
☐					
☐					
☐					
☐					
☐					
☐					
☐					
☐					
☐					
☐					
☐					
☐					
☐					
☐					

Guest list

RSVP	Guest	Bringing	Requests	Adults	Children
☐					
☐					
☐					
☐					
☐					
☐					
☐					
☐					
☐					
☐					
☐					
☐					
☐					
☐					
☐					
☐					
☐					
☐					
☐					
☐					
☐					
☐					
☐					
☐					

Guest list

RSVP	Guest	Bringing	Requests	Adults	Children
☐					
☐					
☐					
☐					
☐					
☐					
☐					
☐					
☐					
☐					
☐					
☐					
☐					
☐					
☐					
☐					
☐					
☐					
☐					
☐					
☐					
☐					
☐					

Notes

Notes

Notes

Notes

Notes

Notes

Notes

Thanks
giving

Thanks
giving

Thanks giving

Thanks-giving

Thanks-giving

Memories

Memories

Memories

Memories

Memories

Memories